The story of biltong

CW00544336

MADE IN SOUTH AFRICA

Lynn Barnes

Words that are in bold, like **this**, are explained in the Word help, on the page and at the end of the book.

The *Made in South Africa* series is published by
Awareness Publishing Group (Pty) Ltd.
Copyright © 2019

Awareness Publishing (SA) (Pty) Ltd
www.awareness.co.za
info@awareness.co.za
+27 (0)86 110 1491
www.facebook.com/AwarenessPublishing

All rights reserved. No part of this publication may be reproduced in any form
without written permission from the publisher, except by a reviewer.

First edition 2019

The story of biltong by Lynn Barnes
ISBN 978-1-77008-991-4

Summary: A simple introduction to what biltong is, some details of its history, different types of biltong, and how to make it.

Book design: Richard Keenan-Smith and Elizabeth Barnard

Editorial credits: Managing editor: Monique le Riché; Copy editor: Danya Ristić-Schacherl; Picture editors: Anne Laing and Lawrence Frank

Picture credits: Cover © Anne Laing; cover (background) © Charlesdrakew / Wikipedia; cover (flag) © Kurt / Dreamstime; endpapers © AAI FotoStock SA / Alamy / Edd Westmacott; p4 © stockbp / Fotolia; p6 © Gallo Images / Getty Images / Nat Farbman; p8 (top) © Iziko Museums of Cape Town / Africa Media Online; p8 (bottom) © Gallo Images / Getty Images / Universal History Archive; p10 (map) © Discott / Wikipedia / Brown Reference Group; p11 © Gallo Images / Getty Images / DeAgostini; p12 © Tom Tietz / iStock; p14 © fouroaks / depositphotos; p16 © benniesbiltongspices.com; p18 © tumdee / iStock; p19 (left) © SvetlanaK / iStock; p19 (middle) © John Phelan / Wikipedia; p19 (right) © sommai / Fotolia; p20 (all) © Anne Laing; p22 © Anne Laing; p24 © Anne Laing; p26 © Anne Laing; p28 © Gallo Images / Getty Images / Ian O'Leary; p29 © Jan van der Poll; p30 © Edward Westmacott / Fotolia; p32 © AAI FotoStock SA / Alamy / frans lemmens; p34 © Heidi Jansen / Bigstock

1 3 5 7 9 0 8 6 4 2

Contents

Biltong can be sliced into small pieces to make it easier to eat.

What is biltong?

Biltong is meat that has been dried and treated in a special way to stop it from going bad. It is very popular in South Africa.

Hunters hanging meat out to dry in the hot sun.

Keeping meat from the hunt

The first people living in southern Africa, such as the Khoikhoi, hunted wild animals for meat to eat. They could not always eat a whole large animal at once, so they had to find a way to **preserve** the meat. They sliced it into strips, rubbed salt on it and hung it up to dry in the sun.

Word help

preserve: to treat something to stop it from rotting, or going bad, so you can keep it for a long time

A picture done in 1780, showing ships from Europe arriving at the Cape Colony.

A picture of a European man hunting wild buck.

European settlers

In the 1600s people came from Europe to settle in southern Africa. They started farms, but they also hunted wild animals for food.

The weather was often hot and fridges had not yet been invented. So the settlers had to find a way to preserve the meat. Like the Khoikhoi they dried the meat, but they also added vinegar and spices such as pepper and coriander to improve the taste.

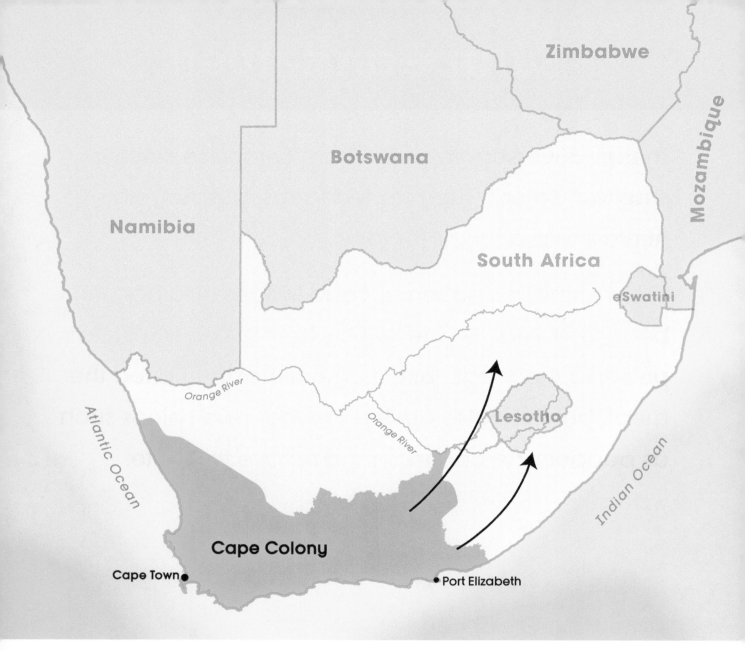

A map showing how people moved away from the Cape Colony on The Great Trek.

The Great Trek

The area where people from Europe settled at the Cape of Good Hope was called the Cape Colony. At first it was ruled by the Dutch, but in the early 1800s the British took it over. Many of the Dutch settlers were not happy with this. They decided to move to the central part of the country, where they could rule themselves.

They set off in wooden wagons pulled by oxen. Their long and dangerous journey was called The Great Trek.

A picture of people crossing a river with their wooden wagons during The Great Trek.

rump

Meat from the rump of an eland makes good biltong.

Food for the journey

The people on The Great Trek needed to take food that would last for a long time on the journey. So before they set off they preserved plenty of meat and hung it up to dry for two weeks. Then they packed it in cloth bags.

They called this dried meat biltong. The name comes from the Dutch language, *bil* meaning **"buttocks"** or **"rump"** and *tong* meaning a "strip". So biltong means a strip of meat.

> **Word help**
>
> **buttocks** or **rump:** the part of an animal where the back meets the back legs; the meat from this part of the animal usually has very little fat

Fish drying out to make fish biltong. In South
Africa these are also called *bokkoms*.

Biltong now

In the old days, when people hunted for their food, biltong was usually made from the meat of wild animals such as eland, kudu or springbok.

Nowadays, biltong is often made from beef, because it is cheaper. But biltong can also be made from chicken, turkey, ostrich and even fish.

Many people have a secret mix of spices
for making their own biltong.

Biltong recipes

There are many recipes for making biltong. The Khoikhoi had only salt from the sea and sunshine for drying the meat. The settlers who arrived later were able to use wine and vinegar from the grape farms, and spices that they got from trading with the countries of the East.

The French and Dutch people in the Cape Colony all had their own favourite recipes. These were often kept secret and handed down from parents to their children.

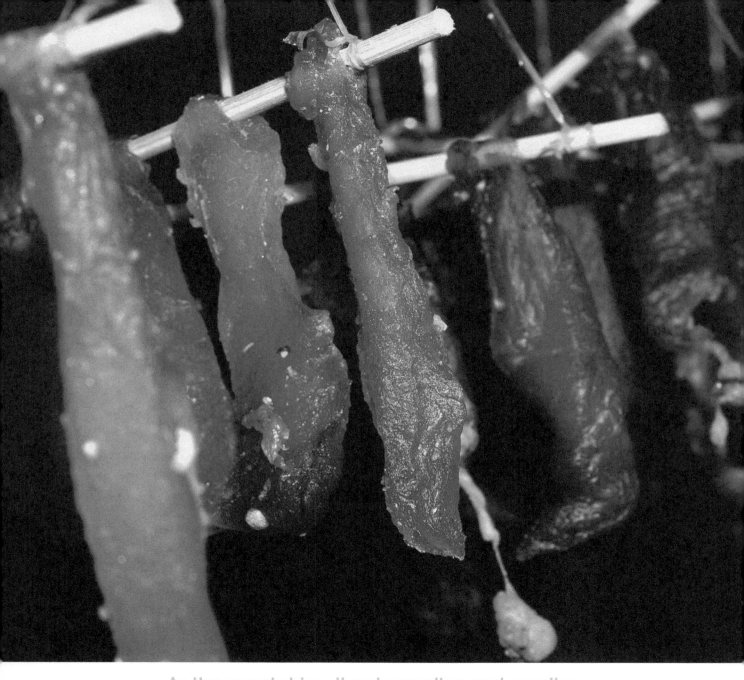
As the meat dries, it gets smaller and smaller.

Make your own biltong

This is a basic recipe for biltong. You could add other flavourings, such as garlic, onion powder, chilli powder and other spices to make your own secret recipe!

You will need a piece of **lean** meat. Very fatty meat will not work well

Word help

lean: with little or no fat

because it may go bad during the drying process. The meat will get smaller as it dries, so the amount of biltong you get will be less than the amount of meat you start with.

Flavourings such as garlic, onion powder and chilli powder.

Wash the meat.

Cut off any extra fat.

Then cut the meat into slices.

Preparing the meat

If you would like to try making your own biltong, it is very important that you find an adult to help you. Using knives and electricity can be dangerous.

Wash the meat. Cut off any fat from the outside of the piece. Then cut the

Important
Remember to get an adult to help you.

meat into strips about 1 to 2 centimetres thick and 20 centimetres long. If the strips are too thick, they will take too long to dry.

Pour vinegar over the meat.

Soaking the meat

Soak the strips of meat in vinegar for a few hours. You can use any kind of vinegar, such as grape or wine vinegar, balsamic vinegar or apple cider vinegar.

Then remove the strips of meat from the vinegar.

Mix the flavourings together and then rub the mixture onto the meat.

Adding the flavourings

Mix together equal amounts of salt, black pepper, brown sugar, coriander seeds and braai spice (shops sell different kinds of this spice). If you want to add your own secret flavourings, now is the time to do it. Sprinkle the mixture over the strips of meat and rub it in.

Leave the meat for a few more hours and then pour off any liquid from around the meat.

The meat is now ready for drying.

Now your biltong is ready to hang up to dry.

Drying the meat

Make a small hole in one end of each strip of meat. Put hooks or pieces of string through the holes so you can hang the meat up.

There are many ways to dry your meat, but it needs to be in a dry place where it will be protected from flies and other insects.

One way is to hang the meat near a light bulb and a small fan. Turn on both the fan and the light and leave for 4 to 7 days.

You can even dry your biltong in an electric oven.

Other ways of drying the meat

You can dry the meat more quickly in an electric oven. Hang the strips from the shelves in the oven and turn the oven on very low (about 50 degrees **Celsius**, or as low as possible). Leave for about 4 hours with the oven door slightly open.

Word help

Celsius: a scale for measuring temperature

There are also special biltong makers available in shops. These protect the meat and allow you to control the heat for drying it.

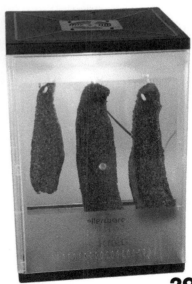

Meat hanging up to dry in a biltong maker.

Biltong *stokkies.*

Types of biltong

Shops in South Africa sell many types of biltong. It can be made from different meats. Some is wetter and some is drier. Some has more fat than others.

Some biltong is sold in strips called *stokkies*, which means "little sticks". Other kinds are cut into small pieces.

Everyone has their favourite kind.

A man selling biltong to people on the street.

Biltong for everyone

Lots of people in South Africa love biltong. It is popular as a snack because it is tasty and easy to carry around.

Many people like to chew on biltong while they are watching sport on television.

Some people give biltong to babies. They believe that chewing on a stick of biltong helps with the pain when babies are getting their teeth.

Biltong is very popular in South Africa.

Word help

buttocks or **rump:** the part of an animal where the back meets the back legs; the meat from this part of the animal usually has very little fat

Celsius: a scale for measuring temperature

lean: with little or no fat

preserve: to treat something to stop it from rotting, or going bad, so you can keep it for a long time

Lightning Source UK Ltd.
Milton Keynes UK
UKHW051844020720
365931UK00004B/72